Pen Portraits in Proverbs

Pen Portraits in Proverbs

by

John Scarsbrook

PRECIOUS SEED PUBLICATIONS

© Copyright Precious Seed Publications 2020
34 Metcalfe Avenue, Killamarsh, Sheffield, S21 1HW, UK

First published August 2020

ISBN 978-1-913113-06-3

Printed in the UK

Foreword

One of the telling phrases that the late Jack Hunter was known for was, 'let's turn to the clean part of our Bibles'. He was referring, of course, to sections of the Old Testament that many of us neglect to read regularly, and his comment was telling. The book of Proverbs may well be one such book! As a collection of what appears to be simple proverbs, or pithy statements, many, even of the diligent readers, give up the task beyond chapter 8. This is why I commend this book to the reader.

Starting with a consideration of the main theme – wisdom – and its importance to every believer, John then directs our thoughts to the purpose of the book. It is written to 'my son', which, as the writer states, 'furnishes "sons" of all ages with an invaluable guide to life'. Even though the material may be nearly 3000 years old, warnings about the dangers of bad company and peer pressure are timeless, and this is what the book unfolds. Therefore, every believer could benefit from reading about 'the wise man and his companions'.

As we come to the chapter on the talebearer, there are equally powerful lessons. John states, 'If we made it our ambition to promote only that which was of positive good in our brothers and sisters, if our conversation was more of Christ and less of each other, maybe the talebearer would be unable to operate amongst us'. Similarly, though we may smile at the antics of the sluggard, there is plenty to challenge all of our hearts in chapter 5. I could say more, but I encourage the reader to read on!

Though there is much of a timely and practical nature about this book, I might also draw out the devotional aspects. How can we read of the wise man, the righteous, or the friend, without thinking of the Lord or aspects of His ministry? The Lord's attitude towards, and teaching upon, the neighbour and the rich and poor will warm your heart.

I have travelled, and worked with John Scarsbrook for sixteen years as we have served together in the ministry of *Precious Seed*. His friendship and fellowship have been a source of encouragement and support over that period and something of John's character shines through in his handling of the book. For me, it has been a pleasure to read and I trust it will be a blessing to others.

John Bennett
Chairman and General Editor
Precious Seed
March 2020

Contents

Foreword 5

Introduction 9

Chapter 1 – My son 13
Chapter 2 – The wise man and his companions 21
Chapter 3 – The fool and his friends 25
Chapter 4 – The talebearer 29
Chapter 5 – The sluggard 33
Chapter 6 – The proud man 37
Chapter 7 – The righteous man 41
Chapter 8 – Women of vice, voice and virtue 45
Chapter 9 – The wicked and the worthless 51
Chapter 10 – The neighbour 57
Chapter 11 – The friend 63
Chapter 12 – The rich and the poor 67

Bibliography 73

Introduction

The Old Testament commences with seventeen books of history (Genesis to Esther), and closes with seventeen books of prophecy (Isaiah to Malachi). In between are five books (Job to Song of Solomon) which, although they contain both history and prophecy, could, perhaps, be best described as books of experience.

The central book of these five is the book of Proverbs. The central verse of the book is chapter 16 verse 17, which really sums up its teaching and its value as a practical guide for the people of God in all ages. 'The highway of the upright is to depart from evil: he that keepeth his way preserveth his soul'. We are reminded that our journey through life requires constant watchfulness, self-control and discipline. Only then will we make any real spiritual progress. This is the underlying theme of the book of Proverbs.

It has been suggested that this book complements the book of Psalms as being the practical outworking of devotional principles taught and learned there. The word hidden in the heart, Ps. 119. 11, becomes the word spoken in season, Prov. 15. 23. The way learned in the sanctuary, Ps. 25. 4, enables the walk in safety, Prov. 3. 23.

The chapters which follow are not intended to be an exposition of the book of Proverbs. No attempt has been made to analyze or to determine the structure of the book; that exercise has been undertaken more than adequately by others. It is rather an attempt to draw out practical lessons from the various individuals characterized in the book, and apply them to everyday circumstances of life and experience.

Perhaps we need first to ask a few basic questions:

1. What is a proverb?
2. Who wrote the book?
3. What are its lessons?

What then is a proverb? – JIM NEWHEISER, in his book *Opening up Proverbs*,[1] suggests that a proverb is easier to recognize than it is to define. In simple, practical terms, it is a brief, but weighty saying that provides a statement by which one can judge their life or actions.

The Hebrew word for 'proverb', suggests a comparison, a contrast or a parable. We could say that, a proverb is a condensed parable, while a parable is an expanded proverb.

So, who wrote the book? – Although many suggestions have been made regarding the author, there is, of course, no doubt that all is divinely inspired. Chapter 1 verse 1, and chapter 10 verse 1, assure us that Solomon, the son of David, the man endued with God-given wisdom was responsible for speaking and writing many of the proverbs found in these thirty-one chapters. Chapter 25 verse 1, attributes the recording of some of Solomon's proverbs to the men of Hezekiah's day; no doubt these were some of the 3000 referred to in 1 Kings chapter 4, verse 32.

Chapter 30 records 'the words of Agur the son of Jakeh', and, in chapter 31, King Lemuel writes words 'that his mother taught him', and wise words they are indeed. We have no other reference to these individuals; some writers suggest that their names may be pseudonyms for Solomon. Suffice it to say that whoever was used by the Spirit of God to place these writings on record, they have a clear voice to us today: down-to-earth, practical truth; sound common sense, both challenging and inspiring. True wisdom from above that we ignore at our peril.

On one occasion, I recall reading that maybe Solomon drew upon the experiences of his father, David, in portraying some of the characters we meet throughout the book, e.g.:

- Jonathan – the friend who 'sticketh closer than a brother', 18. 24;

---

[1] J. NEWHEISER, *Opening up Proverbs*, Day One Publications.

- Joab – the violent man who entices his neighbour, 16. 29;
- Absalom – the evil man seeking only rebellion, 17. 11;
- Hushai – the friend at all times, 17. 17;
- Shimei – the ungodly man, who digs up evil, 16. 27;
- Barzillai – The hoary head, found in the way of righteousness, 16. 31.

Then, if we seek to discover the lessons from these proverbs, the first seven verses of chapter 1 form an introduction, and provide a summary for what follows in the rest of the book. You would not need to read far into Proverbs to realize that the major theme of the book is wisdom. In verses 2 to 4 the stated aim is clearly seen. 'To know wisdom . . . to receive instruction . . . to give knowledge and discretion'. In verses 5 and 6 the anticipated response is set out, 'A wise man will hear'; he will understand the wise counsels, and attain unto them, or make them his own.

There are a number of ways in which the wise man presents his instruction. Many of the verses contain a parallel thought or injunction. On occasion, the second clause serves to emphasize or add to the first, e.g., 4. 11; 9. 10, and many more. The conjunction 'and' identifies most of this type. In other proverbs, the teaching is by way of contrast, and the conjunction in most cases is 'but'; for example, see most of the verses in chapter 10.

How then can we achieve the high moral standards expected of us? How can we be preserved from taking the character of the fool, or the simple, or even manifesting the features of the wicked? Verse 7 has the answer! It is the key that unlocks the whole book, 'The fear of the Lord is the beginning of knowledge'. The idea of 'beginning' is not so much a time-pointer, but rather expresses the primary, most important necessity if we are to benefit from what is taught; a true appreciation of the character and greatness of the God of heaven, and of His intrinsic holiness and righteousness is essential. The awesome majesty and purity of His being must always be our principal motivation in seeking to understand His word and His ways with men.

In chapter 9 verse 10, we are taken a step further. Here we learn that 'The fear of the Lord is the beginning of wisdom'. Wisdom is not synonymous with intelligence, education, knowledge or IQ level, yet, on occasion, needs some or all of these. Wisdom is the right application of knowledge in every sphere of life, based upon a fear, a reverential awe, of the Lord, and on a knowledge of His word. We recall that ancient monarchs like Pharaoh and Nebuchadnezzar had their wise men, but it required a Joseph and a Daniel to apply the needed wisdom. We are not surprised, then, when our secular leaders and politicians make decisions and frame legislation that is patently foolish and unwise. They have no fear of God, and know nothing of His word!

It is possible to have a vast store of knowledge, to be acclaimed for academic achievement, and yet be unwise in our use of that knowledge. On the other hand, we may feel limited and inferior with regard to our intellect and understanding, yet show much wisdom in what we do and say, as guided by the Spirit of God. A conscious awareness and fear of God is alien to the modern unregenerate man. 'God is not in all [any of] his thoughts', Ps. 10. 4.

Throughout the book we are introduced to a number of interesting and instructive characters. They are nameless, known only by their behaviour in a variety of circumstances. As such they are representative and are placed on record for our learning. The purpose of these chapters is to try and draw some practical lessons from a number of these characters as the Lord enables.

The wise man and the fool are both clearly seen. The righteous man is held up as an example, but the untruthful man also has lessons for us. The sluggard drags his feet across our pathway and the talebearer goes about his pernicious work. It should not be necessary, we trust, to spend too much time in the company of the drunkard, or the man of quick temper, but we need to examine our own hearts as we read through Proverbs. A number of women are found in the book, mostly of dubious character. The final chapter closes, however, with a lovely picture of the virtuous woman, a shining example to all.

Chapter 1 – My son

The scriptures make it very clear that children are God's kind and generous gift. In Psalm 127, we learn that 'children are an heritage of the Lord . . . the fruit of the womb is his reward', v. 3. When Eve bore Cain, the first birth in history, she exclaimed, 'I have gotten a man from the Lord'. Rachel, at the longed-for birth of Joseph, said, 'The Lord shall add to me another son'. Hannah acknowledged God's over-ruling hand in the birth of Samuel, as with joy she said, 'for this child I prayed'. These, and many other scriptures, combine to show that the conception and birth of a child is not a chance by-product of some inexplicable evolutionary mutation, but according to the design and will of a sovereign God who is the source and the sustainer of life.

Having entrusted a new life to the parental home, God has made sure that the scriptures provide instruction and advice for the bringing up of the child. But two other factors come into play: the first, a God-given free will; and, secondly, a sinful nature inherited from Adam. The very best guidance and teaching given must be accepted and acted upon to be effective, and many a broken-hearted parent has wept over a stubborn and wayward child. Many parents have sought occasion to blame themselves, but the Lord Himself, the very best of fathers, said through Isaiah, 'I have nourished and brought up children, and they have rebelled against me', Isa. 1. 2.

From Proverbs chapter 1 verse 8 to the end of chapter 7, Solomon records instructions, precepts and warnings directed to one whom he calls 'my son'. The expression is used fifteen times in this section, which furnishes 'sons' of all ages with an invaluable guide to life. It is of interest to note that although Solomon 'had 700 wives, princesses, and 300 concubines', 1 Kgs. 11. 3, and though he reigned for forty years, we read of only one son born to him. Mention is made in passing of the daughters of Solomon, 4. 11, 15, but Rehoboam appears to be his only son. If that is so, then sadly the wise counsel of Solomon was utterly disregarded when Rehoboam stepped into his father's shoes. We read that having consulted with the older men who were contemporary with his father, he forsook their advice before he turned to the younger men that had grown up with him and accepted their foolish counsel. The result was a divided kingdom and enduring strife.

The training begins in verse 8 with the united voice of both father and mother, a basic requirement for a well-ordered house. We discover in 1 Kings chapter 14 verse 31, however, that Rehoboam's mother was an Ammonitess; one of the many women from idolatrous backgrounds found in Solomon's courts. This may have given mixed messages to the young prince, resulting in rebellion in later life.

Here in chapter 1, however, the voice is one, the father gives instruction, an oft repeated word in Proverbs, which carries the thought of discipline or correction. The mother teaches laws, or sets boundaries for behaviour. To the youthful mind, this may seem onerous, but lessons learned will reflect well as the character develops, v. 9.

The first specific guidance is given in verses 10 to 19, with a warning of the dangers of bad company and peer pressure. There is no doubt that each succeeding generation faces its own challenges. Matters which caused distress and difficulty to our grandparents, or even our parents, are met with equanimity today. On the other hand, issues which seem fundamental to a rising generation would not have featured on the horizon of our forefathers. The internet, social media, smart phones and all the gizmos which are first nature to our children would have been totally alien to many of their grandparents. Yet these are the devices which frequently determine behaviour and attitude in today's society. The concerned and caring parent will endeavour to be aware of the kind of company kept by their sons and daughters, in order that appropriate advice can be given to safeguard their path to maturity, v. 15.

In chapter 2, the instruction is summed up briefly in the second verse, 'incline thine ear ... apply thine heart'. In other words, listen and learn! Most children are, at some time or another, accused of 'selective hearing', but the aspiration of the wise man for his son is that he might 'understand', a word which implies the application of intelligence, discretion and reason. The result of following wise counsel is, 'then shalt thou understand the fear of the Lord, and find the knowledge of God', v. 5. 'Then shalt thou understand righteousness, and judgment, and equity; yea, every good path', v. 9. 'Understanding shall keep [guard, or protect] thee', v. 11.

If the full weight of the Mosaic law in Deuteronomy chapter 21 was applied today to a son who would not 'obey the voice of his father, or the voice of his mother, and . . . would not hearken unto them', v. 18, I fear that the streets would be littered with stones! The closing verses of chapter 2 give examples of the evil from which they are preserved who both hear and apply the wisdom given from parents who only have the best interests of their children at heart.

Chapter 3 suggests a measure of progress and maturity in the son who will 'forget not', but will 'keep' the word of a loving father. He is now directed to a higher authority and encouraged to 'trust in the Lord', v. 5; 'fear the Lord', v. 7; and 'honour the Lord', v. 9. He may also receive on occasion, 'the chastening of the Lord', v. 11. In this he must understand that 'whom the Lord loveth he correcteth; even as a father the son in whom he delighteth', v. 12.

Throughout the book, the writer comes back time and again to his overriding theme which is 'wisdom'. In this chapter, the one who bows to divine sovereignty, vv. 3-12, discovers that there is a blessing in the enjoyment of that wisdom v. 13; its value is far above material worth, vv. 14-16. It lifts the soul above the anxieties of life, vv. 17, 18, and, as a constant encouragement to our faith, we are reminded that creation itself bears the stamp of divine wisdom, vv. 19, 20. In the closing verses of the chapter, the father encourages his son to apply that which he has learned to every situation; in the daily walk, times of rest, times of anxiety and in the normal interaction of life.

Chapter 4 provides a summary of the instruction given in the earlier chapters. The concerned father recalls his own upbringing and education which has stood him in good stead. We are reminded of the young Timothy, schooled in the scriptures from a child by a godly grandmother and mother; later receiving instruction from the Apostle Paul to pass on to the next generation those things which he had learned. Again, the warning is given to avoid those who are identified as 'wicked' and 'evil'. They will not rest unless and until they have 'done mischief' or 'caused some to fall'; they stumble on in their darkness with nothing of value in their lives. Wise imperatives are given to sons, 'Take fast hold of instruction; let her not go'. 'Enter not into the path of the wicked . . . avoid it . . . turn from it, and pass by'. In contrast, encouragement is given, because 'the path of the just is as the shining light, that shineth more and more unto the perfect day'.

Before moving on, the wise father calls the son's attention, in verses 20 to 27, to those avenues by which the adversary can gain an advantage. Vigilance is needed in respect of 'thine ears', 'thine eyes' and 'thine heart'. Warning is given regarding the mouth and lips from where 'froward and perverse' words can issue. With so much on every hand to distract and defile, the advice to 'let thine eyes look right on' and 'ponder the path of thy feet' is of primary importance.

At the commencement of chapter 5, once again the son is called to attend and take note of the father's wise instruction. He is now thinking in the realm of morality. The son is no longer a child, but has evidently reached maturity, as advice is given for the marriage relationship. True it is that when a married couple set up home, they are no longer the direct responsibility of their parents. But godly parents never cease to pray for their families and will give help and guidance if needed or requested, right on through life.

It may be appropriate at this point to remember that those who undertake the work of instructing others should always be aware of their own frailties. The 'spiritual' one who takes on the responsibility of restoring the man 'overtaken in a fault', Gal. 6.1, is advised to consider himself, lest he also be tempted. Here, in Proverbs chapter 5, and on several other occasions, Solomon warns his son and others of the threat posed by the one whom he calls 'a strange woman'. She is attractive, alluring and appealing. 'But her end is bitter as wormwood, sharp as a twoedged sword. Her feet go down to death; her steps take hold on hell', v. 4. Solomon was aware of such dangers, yet, sadly, we read in 1 Kings chapter 11, 'King Solomon loved many strange women . . . he clave unto these in love . . . they turned away his heart after other gods' and, eventually, we read with great sadness that, 'Solomon did evil in the sight of the Lord'.

In chapter 6 the wise man gives counsel to his son for caution when doing business with 'men of the world'. Care is needed when dealing with financial matters, or, as here, the guaranteeing of a debt for one who is a friend. Particular attention should be paid to verbal agreements sealed with a handshake. If it is then realized that what has been done is unwise, every effort should be made to effect release from the deal. In verses 6 to 11, another character slouches across our path; the sluggard will provide lessons for us later, but the instruction given is not out of place in the teaching of our present chapter. In the business world, there is a need to be wide awake, prepared and vigilant. The Lord Jesus warned that 'the children of this world are in their generation wiser than the children of light', Luke 16. 8. A caricature is given in verses 12 to 14 of the body language used by devious men. They will talk out of the side of their mouths, nod and wink to each other, signal to their companions with feet and hands, while all the time cooking up some nefarious scheme and stirring up trouble.

The chapter closes with an appeal to the son, 'Keep thy father's commandment, and forsake not the law of thy mother', v. 20. The instruction given was to become an integral part of life, like something placed around his neck that he is constantly aware of whether waking or sleeping, a lamp, a light, a guide and, if needed, a reproof.

Chapter 7 concludes the opening section of the book of Proverbs, specifically recorded for guidance, instruction and warning given by a father to his family and especially to his son. There are eight further occasions in the chapters which follow where sons are addressed, each serving to emphasize the teaching given in these earlier chapters.

After underlining his former entreaties in the opening verses, the majority of the chapter is taken up with a graphic illustration, or it may even be an authentic incident witnessed by Solomon, who himself knew a thing or two about seductive women! We follow the downward steps of a young man, snared and made captive by a temptress. He is deemed to be simple and without understanding; she is audacious and without shame.

Such is the graphic detail of the young man's fate at the hands and under the influence of this vile adulteress that it could be, and I only make the suggestion, that Solomon is in later life revisiting experiences of his younger days. Realizing the dangers of yielding to such temptations, he makes a final appeal to his own, 'Hearken unto me now therefore, O ye children, and attend to the words of my mouth. Let not thine heart decline to her ways, go not astray in her paths. For she hath cast down many wounded: yea, many strong men have been slain by her. Her house is the way to hell, going down to the chambers of death', Prov. 7. 24-27.

Would it be a speculation too far to envisage Solomon in later years looking out from his palace across to the hill that is before Jerusalem? He would see there the high place he had built for Chemosh, the god of Moab, the awful image of Moloch the god of the Ammonites, where child sacrifices were made and the numerous altars and images raised up to satisfy his many foreign wives, 1 Kgs. 11. 7, 8. Surely, some vestige of remorse, some regret would have crossed his countenance as he thought of the legacy he was leaving. The very least he could do was to record a warning to his son, and generations who would follow, to be aware of the weakness of the flesh, evident in even the wisest of men.

It would seem that Rehoboam, the son who followed, did in fact learn something from the experience of his father. Although he had a multiplicity of wives and concubines, and he 'prepared not his heart to seek the Lord', there is no record of foreign wives, or of idolatry during his reign of seventeen years. The same could not be said of his adversary, Jeroboam, who came to prominence as Rehoboam ascended the throne. His epitaph is recorded repeatedly in scriptural history as the man who, by his idolatry, 'made Israel to sin', a legacy which infected the ten tribes right up to the time of their captivity into

Assyria. How relevant to sons, and, indeed to all, is the closing warning of John's first Epistle, 'Little children, keep yourselves from idols'.

Chapter 2 – The wise man and his companions

Wisdom is a fathomless ocean, an eternal fountain which has its source in God alone, 8. 22, 23. It was divine wisdom that brought creation into being, 3. 19. The same wisdom orders and maintains it, 8. 28, 29. It is a clear evidence of the love and grace of God that He has made available to man the abundant fruits and blessings of His wisdom, 9. 1-6. Furthermore, an invitation is extended to those in need of guidance, 9. 4, and all is given unstintingly, cp. Jas. 1. 5. The world has its own standards by which wisdom is assessed, but even at its best and most noble it is still 'the wisdom of this world', 1 Cor. 2. 6.

When the Lord Jesus was here, the men of his own country placed the measuring line upon Him, the carpenter's son, and asked in astonishment, 'Whence hath this man this wisdom and these mighty works?' Matt. 13. 54. The Jews, in similar vein and with furrowed brow, said, 'How knoweth this man letters, having never learned?' John 7. 15. The application of their own wisdom only left question marks hanging in the air. The reality was that before them stood the One 'in whom are hid all the treasures of wisdom and knowledge', Col. 2. 3. The One who embodied and lived out those 'seven pillars of wisdom' which James speaks of as belonging to 'the wisdom that is from above', Jas. 3. 17, lovely features seen in all their perfection in the person of the Lord Jesus.

Wisdom is, of course, the prevailing subject in the book of Proverbs. Mention is made of it at least once in every chapter. The wise man is seen as the epitome of all that is good, honest and upright. He is sometimes introduced to us alongside his complementary companion, the man of understanding, 1. 5, to add weight and clarity to the instruction given. Then, from chapter 12, we are joined by the third character to make up this 'three-fold cord', the prudent man. Together, they represent a formidable body of teaching, instruction, sound advice and common sense. We do well to linger for a while in their presence.

There are few greater privileges granted to a young believer than to be able to spend time in the company of godly older saints as they discuss the scriptures, just to be there and to listen to their conversation. To discover that wisdom, understanding and prudence do not come as a result of 'much learning' in 'many books', but are only achieved and developed in a lifetime of experience!

We notice that these three companions each have their own particular strength of personality. If we consider, first of all, the man who is deemed to be wise, he is one who is intelligent, well taught, experienced, a man of good judgement and skilful in the application of his knowledge. We would expect to receive from him a whole range of instruction and teaching which would quickly fill up our notebooks! Yet, at our first introduction, 1. 5, he is sitting quietly alongside his friend, not speaking at all, but listening. He has learned that great wisdom is often expressed in silence. In Ecclesiastes chapter 3 verse 7, we read that there is 'a time to keep silence, and a time to speak'. It is the wise man who can recognize each appropriate time, 29. 11; take time to examine the occasions when the Lord Jesus was silent. They are very instructive.

As we become more familiar with the wise man, we discover that he is keen to receive instruction which will be of value to himself, rather than to be constantly instructing others.[2] He does not seek a place of prominence. In fact, he would rather take his place in the audience than be always on the platform. In contrast to this, we will later consider another character, very familiar to us. He doesn't often listen, he has an opinion on everything and everybody, and he is not reticent in making it known. He is considered a fool.[3]

When the voice of wisdom is eventually heard in public, 1. 20, we hear not the condescending tone of an intellectual superior, nor yet the formal presentation of a lecturer. What we hear is the passionate appeal as from the tender heart of a woman, pleading with the hearers to turn from their folly and heed the sound advice before it is too late, 1. 21-25. It is worth noting that, throughout the book, 'wisdom' is

---

[2] See chapter 8. 33; 9. 9; 10. 8; 12. 15; 21. 11; etc.
[3] See chapter 10. 8, 18; 12. 15; 14. 16; 29. 11.

invariably in the feminine gender! Can we, however, fail to hear the gracious tones of the Lord Jesus as He spoke to those around Him, or the words of His servants to saint and sinner in succeeding generations? And, of course, wisdom is evident in 'he that winneth souls', 11. 30.

As we trace the steps of the wise man, we notice that he will never use his knowledge and understanding as a cloak of complacency. He is aware of the constant dangers along the pathway, 14. 16. He avoids those things that will dull his senses and affect his walk, 20. 1. In so doing, he makes himself stronger, 24. 5, and able to launch an offensive against the strongholds of man's wisdom, that intellectual superiority in which they trust, 21. 22.

Perhaps, today, if we were not so content with just a little knowledge, just a superficial grasp of the word of God, if maybe we followed more closely the example and instruction of the wise man, then our lives would show more of the character of the Saviour, our witness would be more effective and our assemblies would be encouraged and built up!

The wise man is one to whom we can turn time and again to receive instruction. Equally helpful is his close friend the man of understanding. The strength of this man is his ability to discern, to apply spiritual wisdom to any circumstance and distinguish the correct path. When King Solomon was given opportunity to make request from God, he asked for 'an understanding heart . . . that I may discern between good and bad', 1 Kgs. 3. 9.

In the first five chapters of Proverbs, the character of this man is being formed. It is a process that involves diligence and application. It involves: his will, 1. 5; his heart, 2. 2; his speech, 2. 6; his emotions, 3. 13; and his hearing, 4. 1. Chapter 4 gives clear instruction for the pathway that he must tread through life, and, in chapter 5, his wisdom and understanding are put to the test with decisions to be made in a moral sphere. In chapter 6, he calls to mind those things he has been taught, 6. 20-31, and with sound discernment he makes a clear statement in verses 32 and 33, which assures us that the temptation to sin in chapter 5 was overcome. Throughout the remaining chapters he is seen as a mature man, able to show discernment and good judgement in a number of circumstances: refusing to enter into hasty judgement against another, 11. 12; exercising self-control, 14. 29; and showing integrity, 15. 21. In chapter 20 verse 5, he is sitting alongside another, patiently extracting a confession from the heart. Little wonder that we see him exhibiting statesman-like qualities before the book closes, 28. 2.

Another individual closely associated with the wise man is the prudent man. His name gives the key to understanding his character. The word translated 'prudent' has the thought of skilfulness, even cunning or craftiness applied in a good sense, as the context dictates. This man is nobody's fool. He is adept at grasping the important details of a situation and acts accordingly, 22. 3; 27. 12. He will avoid confrontation even when suffering insults, 12. 16 RSV. He is a man who can be trusted not to betray a confidence, 12. 23. How much damage has been done by those who cannot 'conceal knowledge'! When, however, the prudent man is made aware of things, he knows the best way to deal with them and will act in a responsible manner, 13. 16.

We see an example of this in chapter 14 verse 15. The prudent man is listening carefully as some information is imparted. Alongside him is another man. He sits with mouth wide open, taking everything in before rushing off and igniting that most efficient of media, 'the assembly grapevine'. Meanwhile, the prudent man will wait. He will weigh up what he has heard, and only then with due consideration will he decide if it would be beneficial to act further. He 'looketh well to his going'; he gives careful thought to his actions.

There are further lessons which the interested reader can learn from these excellent men of wisdom. May we take them to heart and live them out day by day.

Chapter 3 – The fool and his friends

The first man in scripture considered to be a fool, by his own admission, was Saul the king of Israel. Saul was a man who was given privilege, time and opportunity to make something of his life. Sadly, he allowed pride, jealousy and selfishness to control his actions, and in 1 Samuel chapter 26 verse 21, he recorded his own epitaph, 'I have played the fool'. What a contrast is seen in the Saul of the New Testament, who, as Paul the apostle, at the end of his life could say without pride or boasting, 'I have kept the faith', 2 Tim. 4. 7.

In the book of Proverbs, the fool is not seen as someone to be laughed at or dismissed lightly. He is, rather, one who despises wisdom and instruction, 1. 7, and who hates knowledge, 1. 22. It is not that he is ignorant of the truth, but chooses rather to ignore it. Wisdom is not hidden from him, but his heart is closed to it.

On most occasions when we meet the fool in the Proverbs, he is seen in contrast to the wise man, sometimes in his actions, and on other occasions in his words. He invariably carries a spiritual health warning! His behaviour is that of the unregenerate man and yet it is alarmingly possible for true believers to exhibit the characteristics attributed to the fool. How many today are guilty of turning their backs on the truth of God's word in both doctrine and practice? How many, under the guise of spirituality and 'the Lord's leading', have chosen something inferior, because it makes fewer demands upon them? How many, blessed with the care and prayer of a Christian home and assembly, have ridden roughshod over it all and have chosen their own pathway? The book of Proverbs says they are fools.

The character of the fool does not really begin to manifest itself until chapter 10. In the first nine chapters, the instruction of the wise man has a tone of intimacy. A father addressing a son, a teacher to an individual pupil (note the pronouns used are in the second person, 'thee', 'thou' and 'thy'). On a number of occasions in chapters 1 to 7, and more particularly in chapters 8 and 9, the pronouns become personal, as wisdom takes the role of the instructor. The tone is appealing and from the heart, 8. 5ff.; 9. 4ff. How these verses remind us of the loving tones of the Saviour as with gracious words He spoke to those around Him, imparting true wisdom from a heart of compassion!

From chapter 10, the Proverbs, as directly attributed to Solomon, take a more general and impersonal approach and are given in the third person, 'he', 'him' and 'they'. In chapters 10 to 29, the fool and those of similar character are very prominent. The warnings and instruction given cover a number of situations.

On several occasions, the fool is seen in the home, where his behaviour makes his parents' life a misery.[4] The scriptures, not least in the book of Proverbs, are very clear in their teaching regarding parental responsibility. The care, the instruction and discipline of children is of vital importance. Equally so, children are left in no doubt as to their obligations of obedience and subjection to parental control. Sadly, in today's society 'man's wisdom' is considered superior, resulting in broken homes, dysfunctional families and whole communities where the 'sins of the fathers' are wreaking havoc upon a generation of feral children.

As we follow the fool going about his daily routine, we notice that he is often recognized not so much by how he looks, nor yet by what he does, but by what he says! While he remains silent, he is even considered wise, 17. 28! Yet such is his nature that he cannot keep quiet for long, 12. 23; 15. 2. The true character of a man or woman is often made apparent in both the content and the manner of their speech. Simon Peter could protest loudly at the accusations in the high priest's palace, yet his speech showed decisively what he really was, Matt. 26. 73. The Epistle of James is the New Testament counterpart of the book of Proverbs; he also has instructive words, particularly in chapter 3, on the importance of guarding our tongue.

The fool has no discernment in matters of morality. He makes a mock at sin, 14. 9; he is arrogant and careless, 14. 16. In chapter 26, the wise

---

[4] See, for example, chapter 10. 1; 15. 5, 20; 17. 21, 25; 19. 13.

man gives clear instruction on how to respond to those who manifest the character of fools. They are not worthy of respect, vv. 1, 4 and 5, and deserve only discipline, v. 3. They should not be given responsibility, v. 6. nor opportunity to teach, v. 9.

The warnings against taking the character of the fool are like beacons throughout the book. Perhaps the most succinct is given in chapter 14 verse 24. Here is seen his behaviour, his character and his attitude. 'The foolishness of fools is folly'!

Another character, often seen in the company of the fool, is the simple man. In many ways he is more to be pitied than blamed. He is not mentally deficient, but is gullible, easily led, naïve and lacking discernment. He is food and drink to the fool, who finds in him a natural audience and a willing disciple.

There are certain matters in which it is appropriate for the believer to be simple, e.g., 'concerning evil', Rom. 16. 19. It is best not to know the intricacies of behaviour, 'done of them [unbelievers] in secret', Eph. 5. 12. It is not too difficult for the believer to exercise wisdom and discernment, without becoming involved in inappropriate situations. Abraham did not need to visit Sodom to know that its behaviour was evil. We, as believers, do not need to see, hear or frequent many of those attractions which engage the mind of the world, in order to know that there is nothing in them for the spiritual mind to feed upon.

In chapter 7, instruction is given to warn of the dangers of becoming ensnared in immorality. The character used to illustrate this is the simple man. His first mistake is to linger in the vicinity of temptation v. 8. How different to Joseph, who fled from the presence of his temptress, Gen. 39. 12. For this man, however, the lust of the eyes becomes the lust of the flesh, vv. 13-20, and the pride of life finally traps him, v. 21. He is left permanently damaged, v. 23!

In our present day, because the word of God is ignored, there appears to be no ultimate standard of truth. Therefore, with the proliferation of so much falsehood, even in nominally Christian society, souls lack discernment, and take on the character of the simple, 'believing every word', 14. 15. The result is that they 'inherit folly', 14. 18. The only sure safeguard is a true knowledge of God through His word, and the constant application of that word to our lives.

Our final encounter with the simple man is a repeated warning in chapter 22 verse 3 and chapter 27 verse 12, 'A prudent man foreseeth the evil, and hideth himself: but the simple pass on and are punished'. This good advice can be applied to many circumstances of life, and is an excellent scripture from which to preach the gospel; it also teaches us to be aware of the possible outcome of our actions and to weigh up every option before making important decisions. Remember Lot's choice in Genesis chapter 13 verse 11. It seems that he did not even consider choosing Bethel, the 'house of God', but turned his back upon it and his decision ultimately cost him everything. May the Lord help us to rise above the attributes of the simple man as seen in the book of Proverbs.

Chapter 4 – The talebearer

Man is by nature an inquisitive being. Of course, there is nothing intrinsically wrong with that. It is a God-given attribute, which helps us to learn and develop through life and to acquire the knowledge that is necessary to enable us to function as God intended. We can, however, misuse the faculties which God has given, and we recall it was the pursuit of 'knowledge' beyond that which was permitted, and at the instigation of the adversary, that first brought sin into the world, Gen. 3. 5.

We have already noticed in our studies in the Proverbs that the use or abuse of knowledge often determines the respective characters of the wise man and the fool – how they each handle the things which they 'know'. On our journey through life, we acquire all sorts of knowledge in a variety of ways. A great deal is accumulated in an encyclopaedic manner, and stored in the memory. We also learn many things that can be used in a beneficial way for ourselves and others. Or we can use knowledge gained, in a malicious and damaging way to the detriment of all concerned.

The character before us in this present study is neither a new nor an endangered species! When the Levitical law was given, included in those instructions for the daily walk of the people of God was a clear prohibition, 'Thou shalt not go up and down as a talebearer among thy people', Lev. 19. 16. This 'first mention' sets the tone for the kind of behaviour we can expect from those who engage in this activity. We observe this character 'going up and down', flitting from one to another like a restless fly, trying to find an ear prepared to listen to some snippet, some story, often embellished and usually unedifying, regarding another believer. Notice, too, the talebearer of Leviticus was 'among' the Lord's people, not a stranger, but one of the family, a brother, a sister, well liked and accepted. Quite often the centre of attention, he is regularly invited to the homes of others, yet sows discord among the people of God. He is rather like the unregenerate Athenians who 'spent their time in nothing else, but either to tell, or to hear some new thing', Acts 17. 21, or those in first Timothy chapter 5 who 'learn to be idle, wandering about from house to house; and not only idle, but tattlers also and busybodies, speaking things which they ought not'. The context is that of 'younger widows', but sadly, the admonition is appropriate to all – brothers and sisters!

It would seem that the warning of Leviticus was timely, if sadly unheeded by some, since the wise man of Proverbs saw the need to challenge his audience on account of the same pernicious behaviour. In chapter 11 verse 13, the talebearer is seen as one who lacks integrity. He, together with another, has been told of a matter in confidence, something to be retained as a subject for private prayer. The man 'of a faithful spirit' behaves impeccably. The matter is concealed, shared only with the Lord, a burden carried for another. He will, without doubt, receive a blessing. The talebearer takes a different route. Instead of heading for the throne of grace, he immediately charts his course in the direction of another believer. With a self-important air, and with lowered voice, he betrays the confidence of his friend. The damage done is irrevocable. Words spoken cannot be recalled. Of course, he has made it clear that what has been revealed is in complete confidence! He will then seize the first opportunity to tell another, but this time it is a slightly decorated version of events!

We are told that a man, or a woman, is known by the company they keep. In chapter 16, there are principles for godly living clearly set out by the wise man. There are a number of characters here that have occupied our attention in previous studies. However, in verses 27 to 29 a rather unsavoury group is found who, sadly, have no ear for the wisdom given. Here, we find the ungodly man, the froward man and the violent man. But wait – who is that standing between the froward and the violent in verse 28? It is none other than the talebearer, but here in this present company he has disguised himself. He will not act openly; he is just a whisperer, a word in the ear of another, a knowing glance, a raised eyebrow. It is enough to cause doubt and suspicion until his objective is achieved, and he succeeds in driving a wedge between those who were good friends. It is interesting to note that in Romans chapter 1 verse 29, the whisperer is found in exactly the same kind of company as in Proverbs chapter 16; he will gravitate to his own kind.

How sad that sometimes the features seen in this character are even in evidence among the people of God!

Our next encounter with the talebearer is in chapter 18. In this chapter, a number of characters are speaking and we are reminded of James chapter 3 where the tongue, its use and misuse, comes under scrutiny. In verses 6 and 7 of Proverbs chapter 18, the fool is heard, expressing opinions in his usual manner, loud, ignorant and provocative. Nobody is taken in by him, it is all too obvious what he is. In verse 8, however, the talebearer speaks. His approach is far more subtle. His words are well chosen and well directed, sharp and incisive. He knows exactly what to say to inflict the most hurt, to have maximum effect. How often have such words resulted in private tears and silent misery as they 'go down into the innermost parts'?

In chapter 18 verse 8, and in chapter 26 verse 22, where the words are repeated, it has been suggested by some that the word 'wounds' could better be translated 'dainty morsels', RV, NIV. A search through STRONG's *Concordance* and *Old Testament Word Studies* by SPIROS ZODHIATES found no particular support for the change, but, if there is merit in it, then it throws a different light on the verses above. It shows the talebearer imparting some particularly 'tasty' details, readily received by the listener, savoured and enjoyed, ready to be passed on at the first opportunity.

There are just two more encounters with this man in the Proverbs. The first is in chapter 20 verse 19, which gives us an insight into his mode of operation in order that we may be on our guard. Then, finally, in chapter 26 verse 20, where we are instructed in how to deal with this offensive individual.

Secrets and the confidences of others are this man's stock in trade. Without access to these he is rendered ineffective. So, how does he persuade others to confide in him? Chapter 20 verse 19 gives the answer; he flatters them! He tells them things that they like to hear; he appeals to their pride. This may go on over a period of time until the trap is fully prepared. The unsuspecting victim is taken in: surely this man can be trusted, and he is so caring, so sympathetic. However, no sooner is the confidence gained than it is betrayed. The wise man's counsel is simple and apposite, 'meddle not with him that flattereth with his lips'. Don't get involved, don't be taken in, and, most of all, don't tell him anything.

There is a need for discernment among the people of God. We must be able to distinguish between those who have a genuine interest in our well-being, who share our burdens, strengthen our hands and carry our confidences to the grave, while there are others who simply wish to make merchandise of our circumstances.

The final glimpse of our character is in chapter 26 verses 20 to 22. The wise man envisages a situation 'where there is no talebearer'. He draws an analogy between a fire, fuelled by wood and coals, and strife fuelled by the talebearer's nefarious art. To put out the fire or remove the strife, take away that which each feeds upon. How much bitterness and division would be avoided among the people of God if the talebearer was denied access, if ears were closed to his, or her words? If we made it our ambition to promote only that which was of positive good in our brothers and sisters, if our conversation was more of Christ and less of each other, maybe the talebearer would be unable to operate amongst us.

Chapter 5 – The sluggard

Time is a very precious commodity. It takes us from the cradle and charts our course through childhood to adolescence and on into adulthood. Time takes us from the school desk to the workplace. Time measures the development of our children and our grandchildren. Time wearies and weakens our frame, and time lays us in the grave.

We cannot arrest its relentless progress. We have no control by which to influence its inevitable qualities. We are powerless to speed it up or slow it down, but one thing we can do – we can waste it!

The sluggard, or the slothful man as he is sometimes called, is an eloquent example to us of the follies of indolence, self-indulgence and sheer laziness. There is ample opportunity in our twenty-first century society to disengage the mind from reality and be taken up by a world where the idols are sportsmen and women, pop singers and filmstars; a world where morality is dictated by the 'soap operas' and where all are encouraged to be 'lovers of pleasure rather than lovers of God'.

As believers, we should live in the constant awareness of a coming day of assessment, 2 Cor. 5. 10, where we will be called to give account of how we have used those things given to us. Without doubt, one question will be – 'how did we use our time?' Maybe, if we heed the warnings as we consider the character of the sluggard, it will spare our blushes at the Judgement Seat of Christ.

Of course, we need to bear in mind that from the beginning, when God provided the ability and opportunity for man to work, He also made provision for him to rest. The Lord Jesus Himself, who in a lifetime of service never wasted a moment, acknowledged the need for His disciples to 'rest awhile', Mark 6. 31. Interesting to note in passing that this verse is found in the Gospel of the Saviour's unbroken service! We are reminded in Ecclesiastes chapter 5 verse 12, that, 'the sleep of a labouring man is sweet', again appropriately illustrated in the experience of the Perfect Servant, Mark 4. 38.

The character under consideration, however, has no virtues to extol. Invariably, he wants the sleep without the labouring; he has turned indolence into an art form; he allows each day, with all its opportunities, to pass him by as he turns upon his bed as a door turns on well-oiled hinges, 26. 14.

Our introduction to the sluggard comes in chapter 6. We would not expect to find him vying for a place to receive instruction from the wise man in the earlier chapters; he cannot be bothered. When we do finally stumble across him, it is in a chapter filled with salutary warnings, and he is sleeping! It is not difficult to hear the tone of exasperation and annoyance in the voice of the instructor, 6. 6-9, as he suggests that a visit to the anthill may be a helpful exercise for this individual. There, he can learn practical lessons from one of the smallest of God's creatures. Industry, initiative, activity and intelligent use of resources can all be witnessed in the ant. The sluggard will have none of it. His response is seen in verse 10, 'yet a little sleep', he whines, 'a little slumber, a little folding of the hands to sleep', surely, it's not too much to ask? The instructor dismisses him with a final warning of inevitable consequences in verse 11, and moves on to teach those who will listen.

A consistent voice heard throughout the book of Proverbs is a clear call for diligence, an awareness of danger and a need for constant vigilance. The man or woman who would know blessing is seen in chapter 8 verse 34, 'hearing ... watching daily ... and waiting at the posts of my doors', the very place where we would expect the dedicated servant to be found, Exod. 21. 6; 2 Sam. 11. 9.

All this passes the sluggard by. If he makes the effort to work at all, it is 'with a slack hand', 10. 4. If he is sent on an errand, such is his lack of discipline that it only causes irritation to those who send him, v. 26. If he manages to catch anything while hunting, distinctly unlikely in itself, he cannot be bothered to cook it, 12. 27. If he succeeds in cooking it, he is too lazy to eat it, 19. 24. He cannot be trusted with any position of responsibility, 12. 24, and, sadly, he must learn the hard way that such behaviour will result in poverty, both material and spiritual.[5] The attitude of the sluggard also produces a moral deterioration. His desire to have things, for which he is not prepared to work, 13. 4, has developed into the sin of covetousness by the time we reach chapter 21 verses 25 and 26.

In our materialistic society, prosperity is measured by possessions. To this end the men and women of the world purchase their lottery tickets in the vain hope of material gain without any corresponding effort. All they succeed in doing is wasting what money they do have! For the believer, who is prepared to work for just and honest reward, the exhortation of Paul to Timothy should be our guiding principle that 'godliness with contentment is great gain', 1 Tim. 6. 6.

There is, however, one field in which the sluggard excels; he has mastered the art of excuses. He can readily produce a perfectly adequate reason for his inactivity. As far as he is concerned, any progress he attempts to make is always fraught with difficulties, like trying to walk through a hedge of thorns, 15. 19. When it comes to ploughing time, it is too cold, 20. 4, hence no harvest. Ploughing is part of the essential preparation required if there is to be a harvest. Likewise, in the work of the gospel, the spadework needs to be done. The seed needs to be sown, then watered and tended. Is it sometimes too cold to go tracting, too wet for the open air witness? Too disruptive to our own comfortable way of life to rearrange times to meet the needs of the community in which we live? Are we surprised, then, when there is little or no harvest?

On two occasions, chapter 22 verse 13, and chapter 26 verse 13, the sluggard uses a classic excuse, which really takes some beating. He has finally dragged himself out of bed, and peers out of the window to see what the day has to offer. No chance of going out today – there's a lion in the street! He's the only one who has seen it, but he is convinced it was there, and that's enough to send him back to his bed!

---

[5] See chapter 13. 4; 19. 15; 20. 4.

We may smile at such a ridiculous excuse, but let us not be complacent. How many believers work conscientiously from Monday to Friday? On Saturday, they cut the grass, clean the car and go to the shops. On Sunday, they wake up with a headache, so cannot possibly go to the assembly meetings.

We read the missionary reports and think how wonderful it is to hear of Africans walking for three days through the bush to sit on planks of wood and listen to the scriptures being taught for hours at a time. By contrast, we cannot make the effort to get in our air-conditioned cars and drive ten miles on a Saturday evening to support the neighbouring assembly and enjoy the ministry of the word of God! – Oh, there is always a perfectly good reason why we couldn't make it! So many of us can relate to the lawyer in Luke chapter 10 verse 29, always 'willing to justify ourselves'.

Before we leave the slothful man to his reveries, we can take a walk past his property, 24. 30-34, that God given inheritance, which is his to work upon, develop and enjoy. It is overgrown with thorns and nettles. Instead of a fruitful field, there is only evidence of the curse. Instead of a well-maintained wall of protection and separation, all is broken down.

We do well to consider our own inheritance, those blessings which are ours in Christ, given richly for our enjoyment, 1 Tim. 6. 17. Do we neglect them, or do we nurture them? Do those blessings bear fruit, or, as others look on our lives, do they, with a sad shake of the head, 'consider it well, look upon it, and receive instruction', 24. 32.

Chapter 6 – The proud man

All sin is abhorrent to the mind of God, and totally foreign to the divine nature. In view of this, it would seem perfectly reasonable to ask why is it that the sin of pride in particular calls forth such censure on a number of occasions in the word of God? For example, in Proverbs chapter 6 verses 16 to 19, the wise man highlights a number of sinful actions, which we are assured 'the Lord hates'. The expression 'six things . . . yea seven' would suggest that the list is not exhaustive, but in prominent first place is 'a proud look'. In chapter 16 verse 5, the proud man is condemned as 'an abomination to the Lord' and in the New Testament both James, in chapter 4 verse 6, and Peter in his first Epistle chapter 5 verse 5, quoting from the Septuagint rendering of Proverbs chapter 3 verse 34, remind us that 'God resisteth [stands against to oppose] the proud'.

Could it be that each manifestation of pride recalls that occasion when Lucifer, son of the morning, declared, 'I will ascend into heaven . . . I will be like the most High', Isa. 14. 12-15? Or when sin entered the world through the desire of our first parents to 'be as God'? If that is so, we can readily understand why a holy God is so opposed to every manifestation of pride in the heart of man; pride is a direct challenge to the sovereignty of God.

It was pride in Cain's heart, when he saw that Abel's offering was accepted and his own rejected, that led to the first murder, Gen. 4. 8. Pride was behind the rebellion of Korah, Num. 16. 3, the reason for the rejection of Saul, 1 Sam. 15. 17 and the psychotic behaviour of Haman, Esther 5-6. Pride brought Nebuchadnezzar low, Dan. 4. 30, and Herod even lower, Acts 12. 23! It was the proud leaders of the nation who despised 'the carpenter's son', who looked down on 'the Nazarene', who, in their hearts, were saying like the men in the parable, 'we will not have this man to reign over us', Luke. 19. 14.

If we are honest, we would all have to admit to owning some element of pride. It is an endemic trait of the old nature. The book of Proverbs, however, leaves us in no doubt that pride is not something to be treated lightly, or dismissed as irrelevant. The man with a proud look is closely linked with a number of actions, all of which are designed to hurt others, 6. 17-19. His look is one of disdain; he considers himself superior. He has no intention of 'looking on the things of others', save only to compare them unfavourably with his own things. He is the Pharisee of Luke chapter 18 verse 11. His prayer will not be heard. God will resist him.

The principle of sowing and reaping is woven throughout the book of Proverbs. If we follow the man with a proud look in chapter 6, he travels no further than chapter 11 verse 2, before himself coming to shame, literally, to be held in contempt. What he thought of others is now visited upon his own head! In chapter 13 verse 10, the wise man traces the background of strife or contention. He finds that it has its roots in pride. This can easily be illustrated by a number of scriptures.[6] Remember, also, those disagreements between brothers and sisters, which we considered to be just a clash of personalities; the underlying problem is invariably pride!

By the time we come to chapter 15 verse 25, we have followed the proud man to his house. On the way, we passed by the house of the righteous man in verse 6, an altogether different place. The 'houses' in the book of Proverbs are a fruitful study for the interested believer; they reflect the character of the occupants and have lessons for us of practical value. The proud man is no exception. We notice, however, that whatever he has managed to make of his house, and doubtless he is proud of it, he is not content. We see him casting a covetous eye toward his neighbour's property. She is a widow and he considers her an easy target, not unlike the scribes in Luke's Gospel 'which devour widows' houses'. However, he reckons without the One whose eye is on the widow. He will protect her borders; He will not allow the proud man's ambitions to trouble her. At the same time, He 'will destroy the house of the proud', 15. 25.

---

[6] For example, Judg. 12. 1-4; 1 Kgs. 12. 10-16; Luke 22. 24.

In the prophecy of Obadiah, we are reminded of the pride of Edom. They thought themselves invulnerable. They felt secure in their own strength. How foolish! A perfect illustration of Proverbs chapter 16 verse 18 that 'pride goeth before destruction and a haughty spirit before a fall'. Their folly was that they looked down upon the Lord's people, and even stretched out their hand against them, Obad. 12, 13. It is well to remember that none can touch the believer or lay hands with malicious intent on anything that belongs to the Lord's people, without leaving themselves open to dreadful retribution.

Another important lesson that we learn from this character is that pride is a disease of the heart.[7] It is not always evident to others that we may be harbouring pride. Eventually, however, it will manifest itself, possibly just in a look, e.g., 6. 17; 21. 4, an expression on the face which speaks volumes without a word being spoken. An attitude, a gesture that clearly says, 'I consider myself to be better than you'. There is nothing Christ-like about such behaviour. The Lord Jesus is the complete antithesis of all aspects of pride. The words of Philippians chapter 2 verses 5 to 11, which we love so much, show us One who voluntarily humbled Himself, something totally foreign to the natural heart of man. How clearly we see that He was never a partaker in Adam's fall. He was not, as the hymnwriter would have us believe, 'a second Adam', Cain was that! The Lord Jesus was 'the second man, the Lord from heaven', 1 Cor. 15. 47, a man of a different order.

How beautiful it is to follow the steps of the Lord Jesus through the Gospels, to see a true man in whom was no vestige of pride. He was never ashamed of His lowly upbringing in Nazareth; He was content with homespun garments and with the company of those whom others considered unlearned and ignorant. He appreciated the suppers at Bethany. He was grateful for those unnamed ones who would lend Him a donkey or a room prepared for the Passover. He delighted to receive sinners and eat with them. He would take a basin of water and a towel to wash the disciples' feet in true humility, unlike the annual Romish charade at Canterbury designed to exploit publicity to the full.

---

[7] See, for example, 16. 5; 21. 4; 28. 25.

Another evidence of pride in the heart is any form of boasting. On a number of occasions, we hear the proud man as he insists on telling us just how much better he is than others, or what he can do that we cannot.[8] Few things are more offensive to the ear than a diatribe of boastful claims. How much more acceptable to 'let another man praise thee, and not thine own mouth', 27. 2, if indeed any praise is due!

As believers we should ever remember the question posed to the proud Corinthians, 'what hast thou that thou didst not receive?' 1 Cor. 4. 7. Everything we have, anything we have achieved, all our hopes for the future, we owe to Him! Paul, the once proud Pharisee, grasped the truth of this in Philippians chapter 3 verses 4 to 7. Those things that he once held dear and in which he boasted, he now counted as worthless when compared with the knowledge of Christ Jesus the Lord. Again, in Galatians chapter 6 verse 14, his only glorying was in the cross, that which separated him from a proud and boastful world.

As we leave the proud man, we cannot but notice that as he began in chapter 6 verse 17, so he ends in chapter 30 verse 13. The intervening warnings and instruction have been ignored. The proud look is still there, but now it has affected a whole generation! Sadly, we see all around us a spirit of independence, rejection of the word of God, promotion of man and his 'achievements'. May we make it our ambition to always render due thanks and appreciation for all things to our God and Saviour, and to make it our prayer that we may be preserved from a proud spirit.

> 'Naught have I gotten but what I received,
> Grace hath bestowed it since I have believed.
> Boasting excluded, pride I abase,
> I'm only a sinner saved by grace'. [JAMES M. GRAY]

---

[8] See, for example, 25. 14; 26. 12; 27. 1.

Chapter 7 – The righteous man

The righteous man occupies the central place in the book of Proverbs. He is seen as a shining example to the various characters as they move around him on the stage of life. His morally upright walk and his excellent judgement in all matters are the result of his acceptance of the teaching and instruction of the wise man. This man is both a hearer of the word and a doer and, accordingly, he receives the acclaim for his consistency. He is a man whose 'delight is in the law of the Lord', Ps. 1. 2.

There is, of course, only one truly righteous man. The Lord Jesus alone is the one who can fully appropriate every virtue seen in the righteous man of Proverbs; the only man who did 'always those things that please the Father'. It is a worthwhile exercise to apply to the life of the Lord Jesus many of the verities recorded of the character in our current study, always bearing in mind the practical voice, which we must hear for our own instruction.

Righteousness is an essential and intrinsic attribute of deity. In simple terms, it just means doing what is right, and God can never deviate from that standard. The Psalmist David declared that, 'The Lord is righteous in all his ways, and holy in all his works', Ps. 145. 17. In like manner, the word of God is righteous and can be trusted in every detail, Prov. 8. 8, 9. In previous generations much of our legal, moral and educational framework was based upon the scriptures. It is a sad reflection that in our present day the word of God has been marginalized to such an extent that there are no longer clear and accepted standards of right and wrong. Decisions which affect behaviour, discipline and order in society, are made subjectively, based only upon the opinions of unregenerate men and women.

Just as righteousness is the fundamental nature of deity, so unrighteousness is the natural characteristic of fallen man, Rom. 3. 10ff. When the Lord Jesus said to the Pharisees that He 'came not to call the righteous', Matt. 9. 12, it was plainly true, there were none! This was His perceptive challenge to their conscience. He did come, however, to 'call sinners to repentance', and all come under that heading. Yet such is the nature of man in seeking to improve himself while leaving God out of the equation, that the pathway of history is littered with his vain attempts at self-righteousness.

The basic concept, which seems to elude man's understanding, is that righteousness is absolute. There cannot be degrees of righteousness, though we naturally try to compare ourselves with others while conveniently forgetting that 'all our righteousnesses are as filthy rags', Isa. 64. 6. Two examples from Old Testament history will serve to illustrate this. In Genesis chapter 36 verse 28, Jacob compares his own actions with those of Tamar, and declares her to be 'more righteous than I'. In fact, the behaviour of both Jacob and Tamar in the previous verses leaves much to be desired! Neither could claim to have acted righteously. Again, in 1 Samuel chapter 24 verse 17, Saul, on realizing that he could have died in the cave at the hand of David, makes a pathetic plea for his own self-preservation by declaring 'thou art more righteous than I', as though his actions had some merit! He then shows how righteous he really was by continuing to pursue David!

When we considered the wise man in the book of Proverbs, we noticed that he was invariably seen in contrast to the foolish man. In the same way, the righteous man is consistently contrasted with the wicked. The first Psalm is an excellent illustration of this principle which has its practical outworking in the Proverbs. As early as chapter 2, the righteous man acknowledges that wisdom from the Lord acts as a shield for his protection, v. 7, and a clear guide for his pathway through life, vv. 8-12. The alternative route is a 'way of darkness', v. 13, chosen by those who 'rejoice to do evil', v. 14. In this way, we are taken through the book, noting the walk and the words of the righteous man, and the corresponding behaviour of the wicked.

As the wise precepts are set out, we notice that every action, every word, and every facet of behaviour issue in a particular result whether for good or ill. Those of the righteous man invariably bring blessing, prosperity and well being. The wicked man's behaviour results in failure, poverty and, ultimately, destruction. This leads us to believe that the principles of life as seen in Proverbs have not only time but also eternity in mind. Men do not always see the full measure of their actions in this life. There are times when the wicked seem to flourish, while the pathway of the righteous is fraught with difficulties and sorrows. We know, however, that, for the believer, treasure laid up in heaven will bring a just and eternal reward, whereas all unrighteousness will receive its appropriate recompense.

In the central section of the book, chapters 10 to 19, there is much practical truth which can be applied, and many warnings of pitfalls to be avoided. We need to remember that the people who first read these writings were under a covenant of law, given and accepted at Sinai. To live righteously before God, however, needed more than just an external ceremonial and legal observance. It required faith in God. The patriarch Abraham who lived before the law, 'believed God, and it was counted unto him for righteousness'.[9] Zacharias and Elizabeth 'were both righteous before God', Luke 1. 6, keeping the law, v. 6, yet praying in faith, v. 13. The unconverted Pharisee, Saul of Tarsus, lived in respect of 'the righteousness which is in the law, blameless'. Yet without faith he could not please God, but would be placed alongside his fellow countrymen, 'going about to establish their own righteousness', Rom. 10. 3.

For the believer in the Lord Jesus, He 'is made unto us wisdom, and righteousness, and sanctification, and redemption', 1 Cor. 1. 30. We can never work for our blessings in Christ, but, through faith in Him, those blessings are ours, and we are enabled to live a life which is pleasing to God. The righteous man in the book of Proverbs exemplifies that life.

Let us then examine just a few of those features that mark the righteous man. In chapter 10, he is also known as the upright or the just man. The first thing we note is his own assurance of life, he is 'delivered from death', vv. 2, 16, 25. His knowledge of this gives him confidence to make known to others the way of life, v. 11. We are reminded of David, who desired to appreciate again 'the joy of thy salvation'. Then, said he, 'will

---

[9] Rom. 4. 3; Gal. 3. 6; Jas. 2. 23.

I teach transgressors thy ways; and sinners shall be converted unto thee', Ps. 51. 12, 13. Maybe our gospel testimony would be more effective if we really lived in the appreciation and assurance of our salvation.

We also notice that the righteous man has no doubts that his pathway will end in blessing, even though there are difficult times, 10. 25. What an encouragement to believers, troubled by circumstances, downcast and sad, to know that 'the blessing of the Lord, it maketh rich, and He addeth no sorrow with it', v. 22; note, also, verses 28 and 29. These verses, and many others in these chapters, will also provide strength and comfort to a beleaguered remnant in tribulation days.

In chapter 11, we are given an insight into the way in which the righteous man goes about his daily work. A clear lesson for every believer engaged in employment. He is marked by honesty, v. 3, and a desire to do what is right, vv. 5, 6. He avoids situations which may cause trouble, v. 8, and earns his wages justly and conscientiously, v. 1. As believers, we are not immune from the trials that may come with redundancy. We should not, however, find ourselves unemployed because of dishonesty or poor workmanship.

The secret of living a righteous life is found in chapter 12. We read of 'the root of the righteous', vv. 3, 12, and 'the house of the righteous', v. 7. The root of a plant is its life source, and the strength of a house is its foundations. The believer has been born from above, our life source is found in God through the Lord Jesus. We also belong to that glorious edifice, 'built upon the foundation of the apostles and prophets, Jesus Christ himself being the chief corner stone'. What greater incentive do we need to determine that we will live 'the rest of our time', 1 Pet. 4. 2, walking the narrow homeward path, living out the example of the righteous man?

There is much more for the interested believer to glean from this particular character, but we must reluctantly leave him for a while to learn lessons from others whose actions are weighed in the book of Proverbs.

Chapter 8 – Women of vice, voice and virtue

We cannot fail to notice as we read through the Proverbs, that the wise man is totally impartial in his dealings with the various characters brought before us. He is forthright, honest, incisive and clear. We never find him sitting on the fence, or giving advice in a vague inconclusive manner. He deals with delicate and personal matters without ambiguity, and never will he bow at the altar of 'political correctness'!

It is evident from just a cursory reading of the book that the precepts given are all inclusive. Men and women, old and young, educated or otherwise, each in turn will find clear guidance and instruction to apply in the varying circumstances of life. The purpose in this study is to consider some of the verses that deal with matters of morality. To listen as the wise man gives counsel to husbands and wives, and to see the dignified place given to the woman by the word of God; a place which is denied to her by the modern concept of 'equality' and the strident voice of 'feminism'.

In the early chapters, we have noted that the wise man's instruction is to 'my son'. We see however that the responsibility of guiding the family is not solely that of fathers, but for both parents to speak with one voice; the mother's word carrying equal weight in directing the pathway of the children, e.g., 1. 8; 6. 20. Sad it is that in our society, with the marriage bond so devalued, many families have lost that balance.

From chapter 2 verse 16, throughout the book there is a persistent warning of the danger of becoming ensnared by one who is called the 'strange woman'.[10] This woman is determined in her ambition to trap the unwary. She flatters, she entangles like a spider in its web. She has deliberately rejected the things of God, 2. 17, and now drags others down a pathway of immorality from which recovery will be almost impossible, 2. 18, 19. The way to avoid and resist the temptation to sin in this respect is given in chapter 2 verses 1 and 2. The wise instructor says: 'Receive my words'; 'Hide my commandments'; 'Incline thine ear

---

[10] See chapter 5. 3: 6. 24; 7. 5; etc.

and apply thine heart to understanding'. In our 'enlightened' twenty-first century, many men and women have lost any sense of shame. Adultery no longer carries a stigma, prostitution is considered acceptable, just an 'alternative lifestyle'. Yet the word of God remains unchanged, 'whoremongers and adulterers God will judge', Heb. 13. 4.

In chapters 6 and 7, clear warning is given regarding the folly of immorality and the dangers of giving licence to the flesh. For the unregenerate it is the pathway to hell, 5. 5; 7. 27. For the believer who succumbs to such temptation, it results in the ruin of a testimony and, possibly, irreparable damage to the Christian's potential for future service, 6. 32, 33. May we ever keep in mind the exhortation of the Apostle Paul, 'God hath not called us unto uncleanness, but unto holiness', 1 Thess. 4. 7.

Having left on record the many proverbs as inspired by the Spirit of God, it is sad, yet instructive, to note that Solomon, 'loved many strange women', 1 Kgs. 11. 1. How vital it is to always remember, 'let him that thinketh he standeth take heed lest he fall', 1 Cor. 10. 12!

In chapters 8 and 9, the voices of two women are heard. One is the voice of wisdom; she stands in a prominent place and pleads with those who pass by to attend to her instruction. Her plea is all embracing. First to the rulers of the city, men with responsibility who sat in the gate and guarded the doors. She knows that if wisdom is found in these men, all the city will benefit. Then, in verse 5, her heart goes out to those who would be easily led astray; she knows the dangers of rejecting her wise counsel, freely given and more valuable than silver or gold, 8. 10, 11. We are reminded of the priceless treasure that we have in the complete word of God; instruction and guidance for every circumstance of life; do we really heed it and value it as we should? The counsel of wisdom permeates the chapter, reaching a climax with a majestic pen-portrait of the One who is the very personification of wisdom in verses 22-31.

In chapter 9 verse 13, in contrast to the voice of wisdom, we hear the foolish woman. She sits at the door of her house seeking to snare those who verse 16 calls simple and wanting in understanding. We will hurry past her; she is loud and objectionable. She has nothing of value to say to us, yet many of simple minds will attend to her with disastrous results, v. 18.

On our journey through the book of Proverbs, we pause to take a brief look behind some of the doors that we pass. In chapter 11, we have a brief encounter with the gracious woman, v. 16. She is mentioned only once, but there is something very appealing about her. 'Gracious' could be rendered 'kind' and the word is akin to 'beauty'. Of her, we simply read she retaineth honour. The New Testament equivalent of the word 'honour' is that applied to the Lord Jesus in John chapter 1 verse 14 and in chapter 17 verse 5 as 'glory'. Would it be true to say that this gracious woman who speaks no words, simply manifests features of Christ in her life? We pass one more door in chapter 11 verse 22, that of the fair woman. Physically attractive, she turns heads in the street, but beware, her beauty is not that of the gracious woman of verse 16. This woman is without discretion. A friend, no doubt, of the talebearer, she will land you in trouble!

In chapter 19 verse 13, and again in chapter 27 verse 15, we hear the voice of the contentious woman. On other occasions, the same word is expressed as the brawling woman. These are unhappy households; both husband and wife have relinquished their responsibilities towards each other. There is no loving atmosphere in which to bring up a family. No testimony of saving grace to the neighbours. What a desperate need there is for strong, united Christian homes today and families to shine as beacons of light in a dark, dark world.

It is with a sense of relief that we turn to consider more of the virtuous women found in the book. There is a lovely expression in chapter 5 verse 18, where the wise man speaks of 'the wife of thy youth'. There is something very precious, very special in those words. To enjoy a marriage in which, after many years together, she is still 'the wife of thy youth' is a blessing indeed! It serves to emphasize to young believers the importance of being assured of the Lord's will in the choice of a husband or wife, and of being subject to Him in the life together. Such a marriage will be blessed by the Lord, 18. 22.

A number of other women of commendable character have lessons for us in these chapters. We have already met the gracious woman, 11. 16, there is also the wise woman, 14. 1, and the prudent wife, 19. 14. All these and more are brought together in the closing chapter, that delightful eulogy, the glowing tribute to womanhood that answers King Lemuel's question, 'Who can find a virtuous woman?'

The scholars tell us that chapter 31 verses 10 to 31 are recorded in acrostic form, based upon the letters of the Hebrew alphabet. It has been suggested that this is an aid to memory. The poetic structure has been lost in translation, but there is much practical truth here that we would do well to consider.

Those who know nothing about the word of God, yet insist on giving their opinion of it, would have us believe that the women of scripture are presented as inferior in some way! They are demeaned and imposed upon, mere chattels who must remain silent and subservient. Try telling that to the virtuous woman of Proverbs chapter 31! Not only does she embody all the finest attributes of a wife and mother, but she is also intelligent, industrious and involved in a wide variety of activities. In verse 16, she is negotiating a land purchase, and meeting the cost of planting a vineyard from the sale of those things she has made, vv. 13, 24. She is a wise and astute business woman, yet has a heart to love and a hand to help the poor and needy, v. 20. The manner in which her husband is mentioned in verses 11, 12 and 23 would suggest that he owes a great deal to his wife for the position he has, and the respect he commands. This is a truly equal yoke, a unity forged by the Spirit of God. A far cry from the pathetic caricature that men in their ignorance promote as 'equality of the sexes'.

The husband and wife in this chapter provide a number of pointers to a successful marriage. It is a marriage in which there is mutual trust, v. 11. Neither behaves in any way to give cause for suspicion. Each has complete confidence in the integrity of the other. There is a concern for each other's welfare, v. 12, and it is very clear that both husband and wife also have confidence in the other's ability to undertake their respective daily responsibilities. They are not so self-centred that the needs of others are ignored, v. 20, they will make available what God has given to them. Notice too the lovely family portrait in verse 28, children and husband alike quite willing to express publicly their love and appreciation to an outstanding wife and mother.

Chapter 9 – The wicked and the worthless

A Bible concordance or lexicon indicates that the Old Testament word used for wicked is translated in a number of ways, depending on the context. For example, where a principle is involved, the usual word given is 'evil' as in Genesis chapter 2 verse 9, 'The tree of knowledge of good and evil'. However, where man is referred to, either collectively or individually, the translation in the KJV is usually 'wicked', as in, 'the men of Sodom were wicked and sinners before the Lord exceedingly', Gen. 13. 13. Reference to the *Oxford English Dictionary* reveals that our word 'wicked' is derived from the Old English word 'wicca' which has to do with the occult, with witches and witchcraft. Immediately, then, we have an understanding that the forces of darkness are involved in any display of wickedness.

Throughout scripture, the adverb 'wickedly' is used to describe and explain the activities of people and nations on a number of occasions. Wickedness, as a noun, expresses the behaviour of many as seen from the divine standpoint. Only three individuals, as far as I can determine, are mentioned by name as fundamentally wicked: Er, the son of Judah, Gen. 38. 7; Athaliah, 'that wicked woman', 2 Chr. 24. 7; and 'the wicked Haman', who sought to destroy the Jews, Esther 7. 6.

The wickedness of man is a theme which runs from almost the dawn of history when God 'saw that the wickedness of man was great in the earth', Gen. 6. 5, right through to the perceptive comment of the Apostle John, shortly before the inspired writings were completed, 'the whole world lieth in wickedness', 1 John. 5. 19; or, 'in the evil one' RV, confirming the source of all wickedness of whatever manifestation.

Of the 330 verses in scripture which speak of the wicked, over fifty percent are found in the Psalms and Proverbs. These are books of personal experience, with the Psalms revealing the motives, the feelings and the fears of the heart with its joys and sorrows, while Proverbs gives wise counsel to ensure the best practical outworking of these emotions. The amount of time taken in these books to warn of those who practice wickedness, serves to emphasize the vulnerability of the heart when tempted by the adversary. How timely is Paul's warning to the Ephesians, to 'put on the whole armour of God, that ye may be able to stand against the wiles of the devil', Eph. 6. 11.

Our first encounter in the book of Proverbs with one who is considered wicked is found in chapter 2, and sets the scene for many of the warnings which follow. The wise man is instructing his son on the virtues of wisdom and understanding. Discretion, he says, 'shall preserve thee, understanding shall keep thee', 2. 11. They will provide the necessary protection from, 'the way of the evil man, from the man that speaketh froward things; who leave the paths of uprightness, to walk in the ways of darkness; who rejoice to do evil, and delight in the frowardness of the wicked', 2. 12-14. 'Froward' is an archaic English word which literally means 'to go backwards'; one who is perverse, contrary, obstinate, going against that which is right and good. Such behaviour is the territory of the wicked.

Before the chapter closes, assurance is given that righteousness will inevitably prevail, v. 21. 'But the wicked shall be cut off from the earth, and the transgressors shall be rooted out of it', v. 22.

In chapter 4, the path, or way, of the one who embraces the counsels of wisdom is seen in contrast to that taken by those who are deemed wicked. For the one who hears and receives instruction, his way is right, his path unrestricted and he can run without fear of falling, vv. 11, 12. His course is well lit and seems to grow brighter as the end of the journey draws nearer, v. 18. This does not mean, of course, that the believer can expect to sail through life without a challenge or a disappointment. But when the darker times come, there is One to support, to guide, to comfort and, if necessary, to carry those who trust in Him home to that glorious inheritance, 3. 35.

The alternative pathway is that of the wicked. The wise man's advice is to do everything possible to steer clear of this way, attractive though it may seem. Multiplied warnings are posted, leaving no room for ambiguity. 'Enter not... go not... avoid it... pass not by it... turn from it, and pass away', vv. 14, 15. Those who habitually frequent the wrong way do not rest unless they are making trouble, and only get a good night's sleep if they have made life miserable for someone else, v. 16. In contrast to the heavenly light which illuminates the path of the just, 'the way of the wicked is as darkness' and they stumble along it, indifferent to its dangers, v. 19.

The voice of wisdom is heard throughout the central section of the book and, in chapter 9, provision is made for all who will hear and benefit by the wise instruction. Nor is it limited to those who are educated and intellectual, but her instruction reaches out to the simple and those who lack understanding, v. 4. Inevitably, we notice, however, that others are attracted by the voice sounding out from the high place of the city. There is the scorner who only comes to mock, the foolish, literally, empty-headed, brainless man is there, and, of course, the wicked man is hovering close by, to see if he can make mischief. Any word of rebuke for this trio of ne'er-do-wells will only result in abuse and hostility. Thankfully, there are others who will heed the words of wisdom and reap the benefit, vv. 5-9.

Chapters 10 to 15 are almost entirely taken up with a series of contrasts, indicated by the little conjunction 'but'. If the wise man simply listed the vices and failures of the wicked man with their corresponding appropriate recompense, the chapters would make depressing and dismal reading. However, for each negative word and action, there is a positive parallel virtue to encourage and challenge the reader.

The precepts in these chapters show how futile and wasted are the lives and activities of those seen to be wicked. Their ill-gotten gains are of no benefit, 10. 2, 3; they leave no lasting legacy of any value, v. 7, 'The memory of the just is blessed: but the name of the wicked shall rot'. Someone has said that 'men now call their sons Paul, but they call their dogs Nero'. They live in an atmosphere of violence, hatred and strife; an early death should come as no surprise, vv. 27, 28, and this is welcomed by the people at large, 11. 10.

There are almost ninety references in the book of Proverbs to individuals or groups who are called 'wicked'. Their activities, motives and language are all considered and, in every case, there is an appropriate word of warning. Usually contrasted with the righteous man, counsel is given on how to recognize and how to react when faced with those who show evidence of wickedness in all walks of life. As occasion demands, the wise man considers the house of the wicked, his words, his thoughts, his soul, his counsels and expectations, each with their attendant threat to the unwary soul.

We do need to remember, however, that all men need a Saviour, even those who seem, at times, to be beyond reach. The Psalmist is right in stating unambiguously that the unrepentant wicked will be 'turned into hell', Ps. 9. 17. But such is the grace, mercy and longsuffering of our God, that Isaiah can record with equivalent certainty, 'Let the wicked forsake his way, and the unrighteous man his thoughts: and let him return unto the Lord, and he will have mercy upon him: and to our God, for he will abundantly pardon', Isa. 55. 7.

Another character who will often be found in the company of the wicked man is the scorner. He is far less subtle and likes his opinions to be heard; we do not intend to linger in his company. He is a mocker; he will not listen to advice, 13. 1; 15. 12; consequently, he is devoid of wisdom 14. 6. Punishment has no effect upon him, though it may benefit others, 19. 25; 21. 11. There are no redeeming features about this man; he is unregenerate, awaiting only judgement, 19. 29. The man who devises wickedness often uses a cloke of respectability, but at heart he is deceitful, he lays traps, he is devious and dishonest. The scorner, however, trades in words rather than actions. This man likes an audience and his opinions are usually accompanied by laughter and mockery. We meet him in the workplace, on the doorstep, in the schools and universities and, perhaps, in our streets. The open-air witness is fair game to this man. He will soon expose 'the foolishness of preaching'. Why should these 'weirdoes' try and impose their ideas on others and, anyway, the Bible is just fables and fairy stories!

The callous voice of the scorner is heard throughout the Proverbs; he persistently resists any who seek to rebuke him. He is only interested in his own opinion and is never hesitant in making it known, 9. 7, 8. Although the book of Proverbs is the place where we find most references to this objectionable character, his like is evident on a number of occasions in scripture and throughout history.

A similar spirit was evident in the young men who mocked Elisha in 2 Kings chapter 2, with fatal results! On the eve of the captivity, the nation was reminded that they had 'mocked the messengers of God, despised His word and misused His prophets, until . . . there was no remedy', 2 Chr. 36. 16. On returning from Babylon, Nehemiah faced the same opposition, as Sanballat, raising his voice in mockery and derision cried, 'What do these feeble Jews?'

Nor was the voice of the scorner confined to Old Testament times. When the Lord Jesus spoke comforting words to Jairus concerning his daughter, 'she is not dead, but sleepeth', the people 'laughed him to scorn'. As the Saviour's pathway approached its climax, the mockers followed His steps to the High Priest's house and continued their abuse. On to Pilate's judgement hall where the governor 'sat in the seat of the scornful'. To Herod's fortress where he and his men of war 'set him at nought, and mocked him', Luke 23. 11. To the soldier's common hall where in mockery they bowed the knee before Him, and on to Golgotha where the words of Psalm 22 came vividly to life, 'all they that see me laugh me to scorn'. Peter, writing later, will assure us that, 'there shall come in the last days scoffers . . . saying, where is the promise of his coming', 2 Pet. 3. 3, 4. And Jude, in the same vein, told of 'mockers in the last time, who should walk after their own ungodly lusts', v. 18.

So, we discover that the mocking behaviour of which Solomon warned repeatedly, was manifested from earliest times and will continue to pour scorn upon the righteous, their manner of life and their teaching, right up to the end times. A number of other worthless characters pass by in the book of Proverbs leaving a stain upon the page. The drunkard staggers across our path, 23. 2, a pitiful sight, destitute and in rags, propped up by his companion, the glutton. The liar, a close relative of the talebearer, makes a brief appearance, 17. 4; 30. 6. As does the oppressor, the man of violence, who thankfully passes by without lingering.

A summary is given at the end of chapter 3, which brings together the characters in this chapter with heaven's appropriate comments. 'Envy thou not **the oppressor**, and choose none of his ways. For **the froward** is abomination to the Lord: but his secret is with the righteous. The curse of the Lord is in the house of **the wicked**: but he blesses the habitation of the just. Surely he scorneth **the scorners**: but he giveth grace unto the lowly. The wise shall inherit glory: but shame shall be the promotion of **fools**', vv. 31-35.

Chapter 10 – The neighbour

Our English word 'neighbour' comes from two Old English words meaning to 'live close to'. That really sums up our usual understanding of the word, as we think of the person next door, or in the same street. The Hebrew word, used throughout the book of Proverbs, comes from a root meaning 'to shepherd or tend a flock'. That suggests that my neighbour is anyone toward whom I should feel a responsibility and have an interest in their well-being, irrespective of where they live. The Lord Jesus illustrated this perfectly in the parable of the Good Samaritan. Responding to the question posed by the lawyer regarding eternal life, the Lord directed him to the law, in which the man was no doubt proficient. Knowing fully the lawyer's heart and his need, the Lord drew from him the quote from Deuteronomy chapter 6 verse 5, and Leviticus chapter 19 verse 18, instructing love for God and love for his neighbour as himself. Not satisfied with this, and 'willing to justify himself', the lawyer asked, 'and who is my neighbour?' The parable which follows is a masterpiece of teaching on a number of different levels. But, in essence, the Lord shows that the lawyer had really come with the wrong question. Rather than 'who is **my** neighbour?' the man should have been asking 'to whom can **I be** a neighbour?' and the opportunities are plentiful.

In the opening chapters of Proverbs, the teaching and instruction is of a personal nature. The father is concerned that his son understands the importance of wisdom, that he learns it and applies it to his own experience. The practical outworking of this is then expected for the benefit of others. In chapter 3 verse 27, the wise man directs the attention of those instructed to consider the welfare of others, 'Withhold not good from them to whom it is due, when it is in the power of thy hand to do it'; the one in need is identified as 'thy neighbour'. A simple, practical illustration is given in the following verse. A neighbour in need of something knocks on the door to ask for help. The householder is busy, or tired, or just plain awkward; 'Go', he says, 'come back tomorrow and I will see if I can help', when all the time he could quite easily have given to the neighbour without any great detriment to himself. Such an attitude does not commend a believer, since we are only stewards of everything we have, 1 Cor. 4. 7. Both Paul and John have something to say on this matter; the Apostle Paul expressed it very succinctly to the Philippians, 'Look not every man on his own things, but every man also on the things of others', Phil. 2. 4. John will write, 'Whoso hath this world's good, and seeth his brother have need, and shutteth up his bowels of compassion from him, how dwelleth the love of God in him?' 1 John 3. 17.

The guidance in chapter 3 verse 29 is sound common sense. Don't make an enemy of your neighbour, don't try and take advantage of him since you are living close by; just live peaceably. One very specific and clear prohibition is given in chapter 6 verses 24 to 29. Do not be taken in if the neighbour's wife engages in inappropriate flattery. Potentially, it will lead to the sin of adultery with all its attendant troubles.

A number of verses in chapter 11 concern the matter of things spoken, in different circumstances and with varying emphases. In verse 9, a man who is a hypocrite, false and fraudulent, speaks slanderously about his neighbour with devastating consequences. In similar vein, in verse 12, a man who despises his neighbour and makes his feelings evident is considered to be void of wisdom. In contrast, the man of understanding holds his tongue.

Neighbours, or those in need of help, are seen on a number of occasions throughout the book. In chapter 16, a particularly vulnerable individual attracts the attention of a very unsavoury band of individuals. Together, they plot his downfall. In verse 27, the ungodly man starts a false rumour. The flames are fanned by the froward man who spreads the accusation, assisted by the whisperer, the talebearer. The matter takes a graver turn when the violent man gets involved and the neighbour who was targeted descends into bad ways, v. 29; their evil mission has been accomplished.

In chapter 18, a dispute is envisaged. Before the facts are fully investigated, one party is quick to give his opinion and state his case, v. 13. In verse 17, it seems that by seizing the opportunity to be the first to air his grievance, he has gained an advantage and appears to hold the moral high ground. However, the other party, his neighbour, is now allowed a cross examination and suddenly new evidence is heard which puts a different light on the matter. How important it is for any who seek to arbitrate to ensure that both sides of a situation are fairly heard. Many divisions would have been avoided if this had been the case.

A very timely exhortation is given in verses 28 to 29 of chapter 24. Here, one has found occasion to speak to another about his neighbour or acquaintance. What he has to say is not edifying and amounts to nothing more than malicious gossip, in fact it progresses to downright lies! This is followed up by threats of reprisal, 'I will wait my time and then get my own back and I'll make him pay'. This kind of attitude and behaviour should never be seen in one who professes salvation. Contrast the response of the Lord Jesus 'who, when he was reviled, reviled not again; when he suffered, he threatened not; but committed himself to him that judgeth righteously', 1 Pet. 2. 23.

Further instructions are found in chapter 25 in relation to conduct becoming a believer toward one who is a neighbour. In verse 8, someone has taken offence over something which has apparently been said or done by another, a frequent situation unfortunately. Hackles are raised, the offended one reacts, only to discover that he or she has jumped to the wrong conclusion, with embarrassing results! The correct way to behave is found in verses 9 and 10. If there is an occasion for dispute or cause of offence with another, then speak to that one privately and in confidence. Don't make a public display or involve others. Else, if you are proved to be at fault, no-one will trust you.

Two more words of advice involving neighbours are found in this chapter. Friendship and visitation are to be expected from those who have an interest and concern for the well-being of others. But people do have a life of their own, and a constant over-staying of one's welcome is not recommended in verse 17. The Apostle Paul warns of the potential dangers initiated by those who go 'from house to house . . . speaking things which they ought not', 1 Tim. 5. 13.

The following verse warns of a matter which has even greater possibilities to cause harm. 'Bearing false witness', telling blatant lies, against one who should be treated as a neighbour will inflict serious wounds which may leave permanent damage. The effect of three weapons is used to illustrate the injuries caused to others by a lying tongue. A maul causes bruising, a sword cuts and an arrow pierces. The Lawgiver knew the potential of lies precisely when He enshrined in the law, 'Thou shalt not bear false witness against thy neighbour', Exod. 20. 16. The Apostle Paul brought it into a New Testament context when he wrote to the Colossians, 'Lie not one to another, seeing ye have put off the old man with his deeds', 3. 9.

In chapter 26, the wise man brings together a raft of unsavoury characters who have occupied previous chapters. We find here, again, very prominently, the fool, behaving in his own irrational way. The proud man, 'wise in his own conceit', struts by, and the sluggard turns over in bed and goes back to sleep. The talebearer is never far away from these unpleasant individuals, and true to form he is found here going about his insidious work. For our purpose in this chapter, however, we focus upon one who is introduced as, 'he that passes by', v. 17. He may seem innocuous, but instead of continuing on his way, he stops to involve himself in a dispute between others that is nothing whatever to do with him. Wisdom says that such behaviour is like taking a dog by the ears, which is just asking for trouble! Words are spoken, insults are thrown and offence is given, only for the intruder to say, when he realizes the extent of the damage, 'I was only joking', v. 19. But the harm is done and he walks away leaving a neighbour hurt and affronted.

The final instruction regarding attitude and conduct in relation to neighbours is found in chapter 29 verse 5. It involves something which, I suppose, we are all guilty of to a greater or lesser degree, both as perpetrators and as recipients. It is flattery. The caveat given is, 'A man that flattereth his neighbour spreadeth a net for his feet'. The word derives from an Old French word meaning 'to lick', with obvious connotations of subservience. Our English word has the thought of insincere praise, with the emphasis on insincerity, usually with a view to obtaining reciprocal adulation or some form of reward. The proverb as given is somewhat ambiguous, with no clear indication for whose feet the net is being spread, whether the flatterer or the neighbour. It could be that the flatterer is seeking to ingratiate himself with the neighbour in order to obtain some advantage, in which case it is the neighbour's feet which are entangled. On the other hand, the man by flattering his neighbour with words that amount to lies and deception is ensnaring his own feet, since one untruth or insincere commendation leads to another. The pretence then multiplies and before long his feet become inextricable.

The Lord Jesus, always the perfect example, spoke words of encouragement, words of comfort and words of commendation. But never would He lower Himself to flattery. He spoke only words of sincerity and truth. When Paul recalled his time spent with the believers in Thessalonica, he reminded them that at no time 'used we flattering words, as ye know, nor a cloke of covetousness; God is witness', 1 Thess. 2. 5.

Neighbours are all around us, people needing help, support and care in all sorts of situations. Above all, they need the gospel, the treasure which we have in earthen vessels, to be made available to them.

Chapter 11 – The friend

We all live our lives and spend our time in the company of a number of different groups of people or individuals. There is, first of all, our immediate family, with whom most will spend their early formative years. In most cases, there is then a wider circle of relatives, some nearer than others geographically and also varying in our affections. The largest group with which we are associated through life are acquaintances. This comprises people who live nearby, those we spend time with at school or in further education, work colleagues and the whole variety of those we come into contact with, from the postman, to the lady in the corner shop, all who may have some measure of influence or impact, great or small upon our lives. For the Christian, those who are like-minded and with whom we regularly share fellowship become our closest associates and, invariably, we consider them as friends. But, for most of us, those we would consider as true friends are a small and select coterie.

A concordance will show that the word translated 'friend' in our King James Version is, with a few exceptions, mostly a word also meaning an associate or companion. The exceptions help in our understanding of true friendship. In chapter 18 verse 24, there is 'a friend that sticketh closer than a brother', while in chapter 27 verse 6, 'Faithful are the wounds of a friend'. In both cases, the word used is akin to 'love'. There may be many on whom we could call in times of need who would willingly give of their time and resources to help as much as possible. However, the ones with whom we would share our inmost thoughts, disclose our anxieties and reveal our plans in confidence, could possibly be counted on the fingers of one hand; these are our true friends.

The wise man is very aware of the damage done to friendship by loose or idle gossip, whether unintentional, or with the purpose of driving a wedge between friends. In chapter 16 verses 28, a combination of two malicious individuals succeed in doing just that. We have met them before. The froward man, in his objectionable way, sows discord. The whisperer adds fuel to the fire and, before long, a friendship is broken.

In chapter 17 verse 9, the talebearer is at it again! Instead of overlooking a failing in another, he makes sure that others are aware of it and, again, friends are separated.

A superficial reading of chapter 17 verse 17 suggests that two characters are in view, a friend and a brother. A closer look discovers just one bearing the characteristics of both a friend and a brother. The proverb is a parallelism, not a contrast. The one, who is deemed a friend, loves consistently in both the bad and the good times. He or she can be depended upon to join with us in joy and in sadness. But when the real trials come, the times of adversity, a true friend will not walk away, but become even closer like one of the family, a brother, or even, as in chapter 18 verse 24, one that sticketh closer than a brother. We surely cannot fail to see a lovely picture of the Lord Jesus in this proverb, the One who came to be the 'friend of sinners', Matt. 11. 19. To His own he will say, 'Henceforth I call you not servants... but I have called you friends', John 15. 15. One who will never leave us, nor forsake us. The joy of Christian fellowship is that our brothers and sisters in Christ become closer and more precious to us than even some of our natural relations.

Chapter 19 verse 4 anticipates a situation which was apparently true in Solomon's day and is just as evident today, 'wealth maketh many friends, but the poor is separated from his neighbour', and, in verse 6, 'many will intreat the favour of the prince; and every man is a friend of him that giveth gifts'. The 'friendship' in these verses is very superficial and even opportunistic in character. Which of us has not heard or read of occasions where a will is published, or an inheritance requires that potential beneficiaries are contacted? Relatives and 'friends', distant or unheard of, suddenly emerge from the proverbial woodwork!

We are reminded of the prodigal son in Luke chapter 15. While his inheritance lasted, he doubtless had many 'friends' to join him in his riotous living. When reality set in, none of them helped him to feed the swine! Likewise, the paralysed man at the pool in John chapter 5, destitute and lonely; we hear his piteous plea to the Lord, 'Sir, I have no man'. That day, he received what the pool could never give him, or even a king's ransom purchase; the voice of the Great Physician met his need in true friendship.

Another man comes before us in chapter 22 verse 11; he is known to be a friend of the king. Not because of any sycophantic attitude, or because he seeks to curry favour and be seen in the upper echelons of society. But rather because he is known for his honesty, his pure motives and gracious speech. Such individuals are rare in our government and among the ruling classes, but the monarch himself claims the friendship of this man of integrity.

We know from our reading of 2 Timothy chapter 3 verse 16, that the word of God is given to us not only for doctrine and instruction, but also for reproof and correction. There are occasions when, though aware of the scriptural pathway, we choose our own direction. Others can see our fault, but we stubbornly refuse to acknowledge it ourselves. This is when a true friend can prove their worth. In chapter 27 verse 6, we read that, 'faithful are the wounds of a friend'. The one who can come alongside and say with all sincerity, 'You are not going to like this, but', then proceed to show from scripture and apply the needed correction; that one is a friend indeed. The reproof may issue in tears and painful regrets, but the wounds are from a heart of love and the healing process can begin.

The contrasting balance found in this verse is a word of warning. 'The kisses of an enemy are deceitful'. There was no friendship between Joab and Amasa in 2 Samuel chapter 20. When David returned to Jerusalem after the death of Absalom, Amasa was promoted to lead the army in place of Joab. However, he proved to be a leader in name only, as Joab retained the loyalty of the army. At the first opportunity, Joab feigned friendship toward Amasa with, 'Art thou in health my brother?' and, taking him 'by the beard . . . to kiss him', he promptly disembowelled him, 2 Sam. 20. 10. An even more treacherous example is found in Matthew chapter 26. Judas the betrayer, having earlier left the upper room, now comes to Gethsemane with a band of men and soldiers. The pre-arranged identification of the Lord Jesus was a kiss, the universal sign of friendship. The Lord's words are a masterpiece of restraint and compassion, 'Friend, wherefore art thou come?', or, as the RV, 'Friend, do that for which thou art come'. Either way, I rather think that from that point the thirty pieces of silver began to weigh heavily in Judas' pocket!

A number of other 'friends' cross our path in chapter 27. In verse 9, the good advice and spiritual guidance given by a friend is likened to sweet perfume, something that refreshes the soul and lifts us up. In the following verse, we learn the value of family friends, those who bridge the generation gap and remain close. The friend in verse 14 is not quite so welcome. He's up and about early and expects others to be as well. Presuming on the goodwill of his companion, he proclaims his presence 'with a loud voice'. The verbal response is, perhaps thankfully, not recorded. The fact that he is 'counted a curse' says it all.

The final reference to a friend in the book of Proverbs is in chapter 27 verse 17. Here two friends are engaged in an exchange of views. Each can justify his own position and, before too long, sparks begin to fly in a good-natured but forthright manner. The proverb likens this to iron sharpening iron, as each is called upon to defend his position and convince the other of his point of view. As a file puts an edge on a blade, so the mind is honed by allowing the indwelling Spirit to teach us, for He it is who 'searcheth all things, yea, the deep things of God', 1 Cor. 2. 10.

Chapter 12 – The rich and the poor

Founded in the United States of America during the 1970s by three televangelists, Kenneth Hagin, Kenneth Copeland and Frederick Price, the modern 'prosperity gospel' has flourished to more recent times through the ministry of men like Oral Roberts and others. The basic teaching equates spirituality with material wealth. If your life is honouring to God, He will reward you with financial blessing and physical well-being. Added to this, the faithful are taught that giving to God's servants increases their chance of divine remuneration. Hence, the media appeals for donations enables the televangelists to own and fly around the world in private jets and travel in the most expensive cars.

The word 'modern' in this connection is something of a misnomer. The Pharisees at the time of the Lord promoted a similar line, and duped the people into accepting it. As the Lord watched the retreating figure of the rich young ruler He said, 'How hard it is for them that trust in riches to enter into the kingdom of God!' With astonishment, His hearers replied, 'Who then can be saved?' Mark 10. 24-26, they thought, if not the rich, what hope was there for the poor? The Lord's mission and teaching reached out to all, but, so often, his heart was drawn to the poor, the disadvantaged, the helpless and the weak. Paul will later remind the Corinthians that 'not many wise men after the flesh, not many mighty or noble are called', but the foolish, the weak, the base and despised, God has chosen. James poses the rhetorical question, 'Hath not God chosen the poor of this world, rich in faith, and heirs of the kingdom which he hath promised to them that love him?' Again, the Lord explained, quoting from Deuteronomy chapter 15 verse 11, 'Ye have the poor with you always' and His teaching was that the disciples had both the responsibility and the opportunity to do them good.

It could be argued that Deuteronomy chapter 28 presents a suggestion of temporal and material blessings for obedience to the law of God. However, this was instruction given to the nation about to enter the Land of Promise. Their national well-being was dependent upon their submission to God and His word. His dealings with individuals within any nation, and at any time, take into account a number of factors, but the words of Solomon remain true, 'Righteousness exalteth a nation: but sin is a reproach to any people', Prov. 14. 34. God will act righteously for reward or retribution to all men and nations, Ps. 9. 8, 17.

It is interesting to note that although the writer of the book of Proverbs had wealth and riches beyond measure, twice as many references are made regarding the poor than those directed to the rich. Also, the general theme of instruction regarding the rich is not particularly complimentary, whereas the poor are spoken of with kindness and pity. In this regard, it would seem that Solomon had inherited something of a shepherd heart from his father. The purpose here is not to engage in the relative merits or otherwise of poverty and riches, but to discover some practical teaching and wise instruction found in these chapters.

The first reference to rich and poor is found in chapter 10, a chapter almost entirely of contrasts. In verse 4, a line is drawn between the lazy man, who deals with a slack hand, and the diligent man, who works and reaps the appropriate rewards. A development of this principle is found in verse 15, where, through his diligence, one man has become rich and feels secure in his prosperity, the other man lives in constant fear of ruin through his own indolence. In fact, in the following verse the righteous man enjoys the fruits of his labours; the idle man, it seems, has turned to wicked ways to supplement his income! True riches are found in verse 22, simply called, 'the blessing of the Lord', that which provides riches far greater than material wealth, and, 'He addeth no sorrow with it', or, perhaps literally, 'our toil can add nothing to it', KEIL and DELITZSCH.[11]

In chapter 13 verse 7, we come across another man, who, by fair means or foul, has made himself rich, a self-made man, who doubtless likes to tell others how he started with nothing. The wise man, as perceptive as ever, points out that if all he has is his riches, then he still has nothing,

---

[11] C. F. KEIL and F. DELITZSCH, *Commentary on the Old Testament*, Eerdmans.

or at least, nothing of eternal value, Mark 8. 36; Luke 16. 19ff. The contrast in the verse is the one who, because he holds material things with a light grasp, is considered poor, yet 'has great riches'. Paul will later write to the Corinthians of his own experience, 'as poor, yet making many rich; as having nothing, and yet possessing all things', 2 Cor. 6. 10. What greater riches can we possibly imagine than those vouchsafed to the believers at Corinth, 'For all things are yours; whether Paul, or Apollos, or Cephas, or the world, or life, or death, or things present, or things to come; all are yours; and ye are Christ's; and Christ is God's', 1 Cor. 3. 22, 23. The Lord Jesus is, of course, the greatest encouragement for those who, maybe, feel disappointed when looking at what others have. Paul writes, 'For ye know the grace of our Lord Jesus Christ, that, though he was rich, yet for your sakes he became poor, that ye through his poverty might be rich', 2 Cor. 8. 9.

Rich and poor are essentially subjective terms. Poverty, for some, is being able to afford only one car, for another it is having nothing but a sleeping bag on a park bench! Society's attitude to both rich and poor is well reflected in the Proverbs. For example, 'the poor is hated even of his own neighbour, but the rich hath many friends', 14. 20; 'Whoso mocketh the poor reproacheth his neighbour: and he that is glad at calamities shall not be unpunished', 17. 5, it seems the emotion of *Schadenfreude*, taking pleasure in the misfortune of others, was apparently alive and well in Solomon's day. Again, 'the rich ruleth over the poor, and the borrower is servant to the lender', 22. 7; and, in many cases, will not be allowed to forget it.

The Apostle Paul tells us that in the last days men shall be lovers of pleasure rather than lovers of God. But pleasure is a leaking vessel and even Solomon himself came to that conclusion, declaring it to be vanity, Eccles. 2. 1. In Proverbs chapter 21 verse 17, in spite of the opulence that surrounded him, he wrote, 'He that loveth pleasure shall be a poor man: he that loveth wine and oil shall not be rich'. The allusion is no doubt to spiritual riches, much of which Solomon forfeited by his reprehensible lifestyle in later years. The warning, however, remains on the indelible word.

Wealth derives from two main sources. On the one hand it can be inherited and passed on through generations, or on the other hand it results from hard work, diligence and careful financial management. There are, however, many roads which lead to poverty. The wise man in Proverbs does not dwell so much on how wealth is accumulated, but rather how it is handled and how it affects the holder's behaviour. An important lesson is taught in chapter 22 verse 2, 'The rich and poor meet together: the Lord is the maker of them all'. In other words, what a man has carries no weight with God, for all we have comes from Him, 1 Cor. 4. 7. It is what we do with what He has given to us that will determine reward or loss.

In chapter 6 verse 11, and again in chapter 24 verse 34, indolence is seen as a highway to poverty. The maxim is repeated to give emphasis, 'so shall thy poverty come as one that travelleth', or as sure as every journey has an end, 'and thy want as an armed man', suddenly, without warning like a highwayman on the road! Another clearly marked path to poverty is in the company of one who refuses instruction, he won't listen, so shame and shortage will be his penalty, 13. 18.

The drunkard and the glutton have also set their compass in a dangerous direction, 23. 21; they are joined by a man clothed in rags, all journeying on in ignorance to final destitution. Two contrasting characters are seen in chapter 28 verse 19. The first man is diligently ploughing his land, ready to plant his field with wheat in expectation of a harvest. His fellow man has leaned on the gate and watched him with a cynical smile. Soon, along come his mates. Proverbs calls them 'vain'. Luke, in his usual graphic way, would call them 'lewd fellows of the baser sort'. They come with a plan to help him spend his money. No back-breaking work for this man; his field can lie fallow; poverty is inevitable.

Greed marks the man in chapter 28 verse 22. He is determined to accumulate as much wealth as he can, and by whatever means in as short a time as possible, a million before he is thirty! But his nefarious practices catch up with him and, before he realizes it as in a previous chapter, his 'riches make themselves wings and fly away', 23. 5.

Almost every chapter in Proverbs has some advice, instruction or warning for those with riches or in poverty. The rich are reminded of the folly of trusting in riches as, at the end of the day, material wealth can only buy 'things' which will all be left behind. On the other hand, the life of the righteous, whose trust is in God, shall flourish, 11. 28. A very significant truth is given in chapter 19 verse 14, 'house and riches are the inheritance of fathers', handed on from generation to earthly generation, but 'a prudent wife is from the Lord'. A search in my concordance revealed that the word translated 'prudent' on this occasion is not the one normally used throughout Proverbs. Usually, it is a word which means skilful or, on occasion, cunning, not always in a good sense. On this occasion, however, the word embraces far more. It involves intelligence, skill, expertise, ability to teach and guide, to have understanding and wisdom. Who suggested that the Bible demeans women and promotes misogyny? Such a wife is valued far above any precious stones, 31. 10.

There are many other lessons to learn from Solomon's wise words, but we will let Agur have the final word in chapter 30 verse 8, 'Remove far from me vanity and lies: give me neither poverty nor riches: feed me with food convenient for me: lest I be full, and deny thee, and say, Who is the Lord? or lest I be poor, and steal, and take the name of my God in vain'. Wise words indeed.

Bibliography

J. N. DARBY, *New Translation of the Holy Scriptures*, Stow Hill Bible and Tract Depot, 1966.

A. J. HIGGINS, *What the Bible teaches – Proverbs*, Ritchie Old Testament Commentaries, John Ritchie Ltd, 2008.

J. NEWHEISER, *Opening up Proverbs*, Day One Publications, 2008.

W. MACDONALD, *Enjoying the Proverbs*, Walterick Publishers, 1982.

E. H. PETERSON, *Proverbs*, The Message, Navpress, 1995.

J. STRONG, *Exhaustive Concordance of the Scriptures*, Hendricksen Publishers, 2009.

S. ZODHIATES, *The Complete Word Study, Old Testament*, AMG Publishers, 1994.